and we, with closest friends.

ACKNOWLEDGMENTS

We would like to thank Harold Pinter and Alexander Solzhenitsyn
for their kind and generous comments but we can't because they didn't make any.

Thanks are due to James Herriot for vetting the entire manuscript and a
very special debt is owed to the Inland Revenue. Also to Valerie Singleton, the
Consumers' Friend, for her seal of approval (we'd like to thank you in person
sometime Valerie) and to Mary Whitehouse for the only dirty joke in the book.

We are grateful to the Chinese Army for the crowd scenes, to the
National Gallery for certain pictures (they don't know about those yet) and to
the English language for throwing up great writers like what we are.

Morecambe *Lancs* [Mawr Cum, "great hollow"]. Mun. bor. and watering place. Ecclesiastical district no 3834. Mild and equable. There are some remarkable stone coffins to be seen. In Morecambe Bay, at 12 fathoms, is Morecambe Bay Light Vessel, with group flashing.

(From Bartholomew's Gazetteer of the British Isles)

Wise [*wiz*] *n* having or showing wisdom; perceptive, prudent, discreet; well informed; (*sl*) knowing all about, Well warned against, w. guy (*sl*) one who thinks himself cleverer than he is.

(From The Penguin English Dictionary)

INTRODUCTION
by Des O'Connor

The famous Eric Morecambe and Ernie Wise O.B.E.s
need no Introduction.
So here instead is a picture of me.

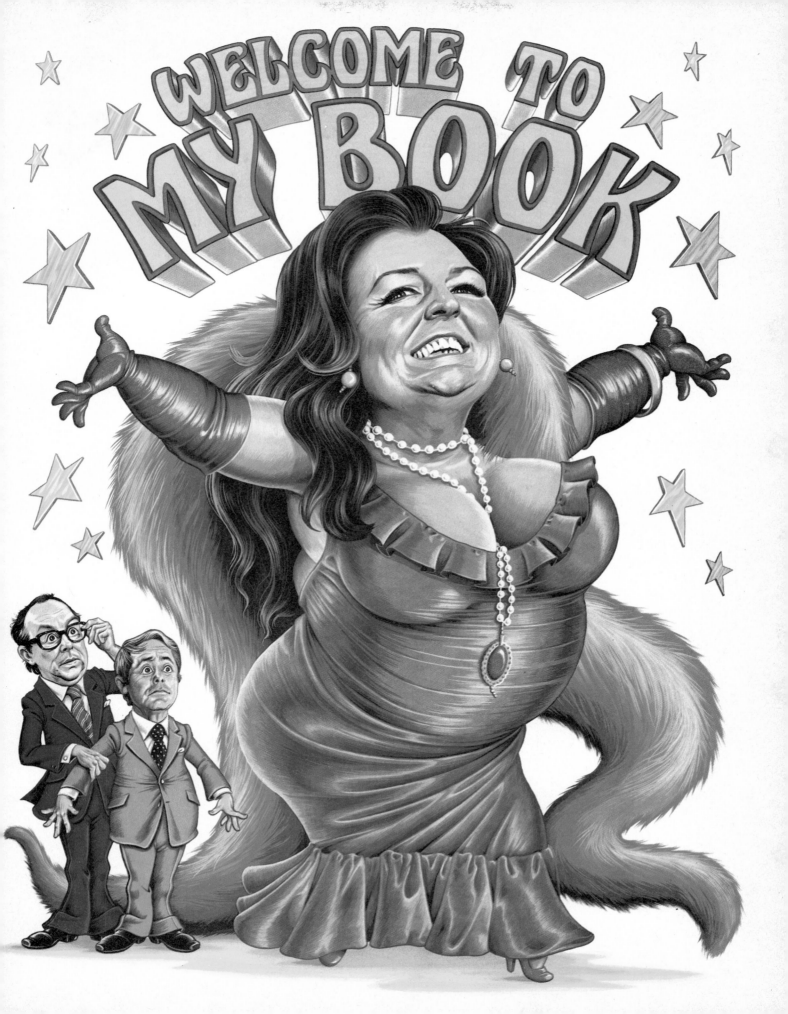

Postbag...

APPLICATION FOR APPEARANCE IN AN ERN EPIC

(Block letters please)
Please answer the following questions truthfully.

SURNAME MOORE

FORENAMES PATRICK (TALKING VERY VERY VERY VERY FAST)

ADDRESS A BLACK HOLE (WITH A WIFE & 2 SQUARES)

OCCUPATION

SEX APPEAL NEBULOUS MARS

FAVOURITE BREAKFAST FOOD ASTRONOMIC

PAYABLE TO JODRELL BANK

FEE PROPOSED

ENCLOSED DOWN-PAYMENT MY TAILOR (ANONYMOUS)

I WISH TO APPEAR IN: STARS ON SUNDAY

2nd. Choice A NEW SUIT

(To be signed by applicant)

APPLICATION FOR APPEARANCE IN AN ERN EPIC

(Block letters please)
Please answer the following questions truthfully.

SURNAME WEDGWOOD BENN

FORENAMES COMRADE

ADDRESS NUMBER 10 (SOON)

OCCUPATION NUMBER 10 (SOON)

SEX APPEAL COLLECTIVE

FAVOURITE BREAKFAST FOOD CHICKEN (RIGHT WING ONLY)

PAYABLE TO MY SHOP (CLOSED)

FEE PROPOSED CARRIED

ENCLOSED DOWN-PAYMENT ONE KITCHEN CABINET

I WISH TO APPEAR IN:

Choice LUCKY JIM

2nd. Choice NUMBER 10 (SO...)

APPLICAT... APPEARAN...

(Block letters please)
Please answer the following que...

SURNAME VI

ADDRESS HALO!

SEX APPEAL

FAVOURITE BREAKFAST FOO... INFAL...

PROPOSED MASSES

DOWN-PAYMENT

...O APPEAR IN: THE ITALIAN JOB

DO NOT WRITE IN THIS SPACE (... ERIC'S USE ONLY)

2nd...

APPLICATION APPEARANCE

(Block letters please)
Please answer the following questions

SURNAME RICHMOND

ADDRESS NEVER WORN...

SEX APPEAL PLEASE G...

FAVOURITE BREAKFAST FOO...

FEE PROPOSED I'D GIVE EVERYTHING...

ENCLOSED DOWN-PAYMENT

I WISH TO APPEAR IN:

1st. Choice NUDE WITH VIOLIN

DO NOT WRITE IN THIS SPACE (FOR ERIC'S USE ONLY)

APPLICATION FOR APPEARANCE IN AN ERN EPIC

(...please)
...e following questions truthfully.

SURNAME ...MAGNUSSON	FORENAMES	MANGUS MONGOOSE MAGNUS	
...ESS DIGS	OCCUPATION	PYRAMID SELLING	
...X APPEAL PASSABLE			
FAVOURITE BREAKFAST FOOD	BRAINS		
FEE PROPOSED ANYTHING QUESTIONABLE	PAYABLE TO THE BANKS OF THE NILE		
ENCLOSED DOWN-PAYMENT PASS			

I WISH TO APPEAR IN:
1st. Choice OPPORTUNITY KNOCKS
2nd. Choice THE INTELLIGENCE MEN (BOTH PARTS PLEASE)

N. Magnusson

DO NOT WRITE IN THIS SPACE
(FOR ERIC'S USE ONLY)

(To be signed by applicant)

...FOR ...N AN ERN EPIC

...lly.

FORENAMES ALEXANDER "POPE"			
OCCUPATION MONTINI PEOPLE			

...UAKERS
...LE TO ALEXANDER VI

...OH CALCUTTA!

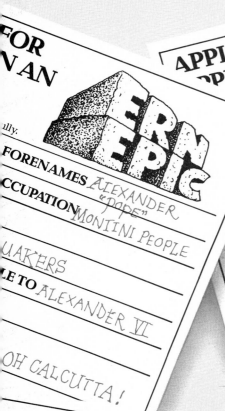

ERN EPIC

...RENAMES FIONA (NEE VIRGINIA)
...CUPATION MEN ONLY

...GENEROUSLY
...ME LAID (HA! HA!)
...LE TO MEN ONLY
...S TO YOU!
...ce NUDE WITHOUT VIOLIN

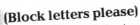

APPLICATION FOR APPEARANCE IN AN ERN EPIC

(Block letters please)
Please answer the following questions truthfully.

SURNAME NIXON	FORENAMES	RICHARD MILLSTONE	
ADDRESS PRESIDENTIAL	OCCUPATION	RECORDER	
SEX APPEAL NONE WHATSOEVER			
FAVOURITE BREAKFAST FOOD SOUR GRAPES			
FEE PROPOSED PARDON?	PAYABLE TO ALL THE PRESIDENT'S MEN		
ENCLOSED DOWN-PAYMENT ~~THE BUNGLERY~~			

I WISH TO APPEAR IN:
1st. Choice THE PARDONER'S TALE
2nd. Choice SPOOL FOR SCANDAL or PLANET OF THE TAPES

R. M. Nixon

DO NOT WRITE IN THIS SPACE
(FOR ERIC'S USE ONLY)

(To be signed by applicant)

Bishop Odour Morecambe
(999-1077)

known as "The Warrior Priest"
and "The Pope's friend" who
failed to turn up for the Battle of
Hastings due to a traffic jam on
the A21. He coined the phrase
"That's one in the eye for Harold."

Sir Jasper 'Needles' Morecambe
(1300-?)

Minister of Health during the
Black Death who lived a very
long time.

Sir Christopher Morecambe
(1600-1700)

who started the Great Fire of
London and earned fame and
fortune for rebuilding it.

The House of Morecambe

Sir Jack 'I'm all Right' Morecambe
(1750-1830)

who fought for Napoleon and
Wellington at Waterloo, in that
order.

Sir Walter Morecambe
(1550-1660)

courtier and seadog who used
Queen Elizabeth's cloak to keep
his feet dry in the mud.

Lord Pullover 'Daredevil' Morecambe
(1800-1900)

who transferred to the Heavy
Brigade during a well-known
cavalry charge at Balaclava.

Eric Morcum

by

ERNEST WISE O.B.E.

When they asked me a couple of minutes ago to write something about Eric, my home help, I said, 'Where's the money?' You see, I do have to keep up this facade of being mean and tight-fisted which has been built up over the years by Eric. Really, I'm kind and gentle and occasionally quite generous with my time, but I do feel that great talent –like what I've got–should not go unrewarded–so where's the money? But we were talking about four-eyes. Well, I first met Eric on the train at Crewe. All great double acts start at Crewe. He was eating his ticket at the time. I discovered afterwards he was nibbling out the date before the collector came. I said to him, 'Why don't we do a double act together? Do you know a little joke?' He said, 'Yes, you.' And that's how it all started...he's been insulting me ever since. Of course I handle the money! We split everything straight down the middle, 60-40. I explained to him I get the 60, but I do have to pay more tax than him.

Somebody once asked me the definition of comic relief. I said when Eric goes home. I first saw Eric give his audition for Jack Hylton in Manchester. He was wearing a black beret, boot-lace tie, cut down dress suit held together with a large safety pin, red socks and holding a large lollipop. I thought, how anybody can walk about in the street dressed like that is ridiculous.

He sang a song called *I'm not all There*, then did his impression of Flanagan and Allen but only did Allen; I've never been able to work that one out. My valet brought him to my dressing room, number one. (Jack Hylton always changed with the band.) Eric said Good God. I said yes. He said, 'I never thought I would be given a private audience with such a great man.' I said, 'Not many people do. Get up off your knees.'

That's how we met. Now my personal opinion of Eric. I've always found him a shy, sensitive person, not one for pushing himself forward. Rather like a liberal–lonely, but with his feet planted firmly in the air. Very good to his Mother; never goes home. Doesn't really need glasses, quite capable of drinking straight out of the bottle. Always respectful to me, he knows his

Inquiring

pensive

vital

place and calls me his little fat friend who wears a wig. He says you can't see the join, that I have short fat hairy legs, and am mean with my money. He cracks jokes like 'He's got moths in his wallet that have not learned to fly yet; he's got short arms and long pockets; he suffers from rheumatism in the right hip from stealing wet change off the bar.' He says I collect white fivers; drink very quickly because I had one knocked over once; calls me little Ern–get the tea ern. Says I'm dynamite with the girls but I've only got a short fuse.

I would like to defend myself. First of all money is not everything–there are stocks and shares and travellers checks. We have never let money come between us. It never gets past me. I don't wear a wig; it's Eric who is going bald. At least baldness has one advantage when you have visitors, you only have to straighten your tie. I said to him the other day, 'You're going bald.' He said, 'When you are losing your hair at the front it means you're a great thinker and when you're losing it at the back it means you're a great lover.' I said, 'But yours is going at the front and the back.' He said, 'Yes I think I'm a great lover.'

The only fault I can find is that Eric is an egotist; he's more interested in himself than me. But he's the bravest man I know. He actually finished a meal in a motorway cafe. I think one of my biggest regrets in all the years I've been in the theatre is that I've never been able to sit in the audience and watch me. Eric looks like an identikit picture of Shaw Taylor. And I'd still like to know what he does for a living.

Egbert Wise
(750-806)

playwright, author of the well-
known Anglo Saxon musical
comedy *Make Me an Offa.*

Lady Godawful Wise
(1040-1080)

playwright, who rode naked to the
Coventry Hippodrome for her
play *Much Ado about Very Little.*

William 'Shakespeare' Wise
(1564-1616)

copywriter, who copied the writings of his
contemporaries under his own name. He lived
uninvited with the Royal Family and was known
to his bank manager as Merry Wise of Windsor.

ThE hOUSE OF WISE

Oscar Wise
(1856-1900)

playwright, whose works include
The Importance of Being Earnest
and *Look Back in Earnest*.

Edward 'Gibbon' Wise
(1737-1794)

whose multi-volume saga of
Italian cricket, *Decline and Fall
of the Roman Umpire*, sold no
copies at all.

Sir Charles Wise
(1812-1870)

author of *David Diamondfield*,
Nicholas Silverby and a *Tale of
Two Banks*.

Eric Wise
by Eric Morecambe,
– I mean Ernie Wild
by… I'll start again.

My little Fat Friend

by the Tall Goodlooking One with the Glasses.

What can I say about Ernie Wise that has not already been said… Very little… And that's been said a few times…
Youm, the people whom have been foolhardy enough to steal this book from your local bookstore only see Eddie Wise as a character flitting on your TV screens. A rather gay little being… whose looks of distrust–his quick nervous giggles and his long-suffering pauses usually mean he's forgotten what comes next. A man whose great performing ability is sometimes marred by the fact that I've tightened the belt on his special appliance a couple of notches…

To us whom are within the portals of showbizz, Ernie Wise is a living legend...he is loved...and envied. Who has been more honoured?

O.B.E.
Freedom of the city of London
Seven S.F.T.A. awards
Two awards by the Sun newspaper
Two awards by Radio Enterprises
Two awards by the Variety Club of Great Britain
One award by the Grand Order of the Water Rats
One special award from the Grand Order of the Water Rats
Six Command Performances
Two special Command Performances at Windsor Castle

You put all these things together and what have you got...I'll tell you what you've got...a crawler...that's what you've got... How many people know that Ernie White is a great Wreckontour. Also a great gourmet...oh yes, he knows all there is to know about wines... I have actually been with him when we've been dining out with some of the Beautiful People of the Jet Lag Set...and many's the time I've heard him say to the headwaiter, 'I'll leave it to you, sunbeam!'

A man about women.

A sure sign of a man about women... Do you realize that he is one of the few men whom can actually tell the difference between a Welsh Rarebit and a Scotch Egg by touch alone... The man has a natural bent which I can verify as I have kept the negatives...

But what you want to know–and rightly so–is what is Bernie White like off the screen...is there another Ernie Wine? Well! Only I can tell you...because I know Ernie Wyse almost as well as his bank manager in Peterborough. First of all he's good to his mother as he never goes home.

Good to his mother.

Who was it who said Ernie Wise is a myth?... Me...it was me who said that...I said it while I was drunk–I meant to say miss.

How many of you people watching this page know anything about his war record?... Probably about two, and one of those had a small black moustache and a stiff arm... During the First World War our little hero had two horses and a nurse shot from under him... And on the day that the Second World War was declared...do

you know what he was doing like the great man he is?... He was at his local saw-mill thinking about cutting his finger off... But he went into Espionage–He thought it was a shop at the back of Swan and Edgar's–

Living legend.

In 1940 he blew up four trains and two ammunition dumps...so then they sent him overseas. After that he came home to his beloved England...and went into Banking and Showbizz. He came into money through a lucky stroke... His rich uncle had one and left him everything...

Rich, young, virile.

In short (and he is) I quote from his contemporaries.

Sir Glenda Jackson
'I'd like him for my key-ring'

Mary Wilson
'I don't know whether he's bald or not, as I've never seen him without his wig'

Andre Previn
'Good God'–and–'Never again'

Robert Morley
'He says he's a self-made man ... and I think it's rather sweet of him to take the blame'

Gayle Hunnicut
'Once we went out for dinner together ... I picked up the bill and he picked up the tip'

Susan Hampshire
'Same as Andre Previn'

The Man In The Street
'Well...eesacreempuffinee'

Lord Olivier
'Mr Wise's writing is riveting, and that's what he should be doing ... not writing, but in a Dock Yard riveting'

Note: Lord Olivier's quote was taken while he was under the influence of a truth serum

The Morecambe

1 'Horrifying'–
Des O'Connor

2 'I cannot think of a
finer man'–
Lew Grade

3 'I cannot fault this
book'–
Ronnie Corbett

A LAUGH A JOKE and A TOUPEE
Ernie Wise

I·SPY LEW GRADE BOOK

Ernie Wise
Small is beautiful

with Tripleday

The AA Guide to Harpenden

6 'Pure
plagiarism'
–R.A.C.

Pole Vaulting made difficult
by Eric Morecambe

7 'Should do
wonders for
the profession'–
Royal
College of
Surgeons

10 'A welcome piece of
grovelling'–
Ian Trethowan

The Magnificent BBC
A sincere tribute to the clever,
generous, kind, good contracts
department from a grateful
Eric and Ernie

How to Dance
Eric Morecambe & Ernie Wise
& Rudolf Nureyev

GREAT PLAYS I have wrote
ERNIE WISE

Bringing up a Pterodactyl at home
by Eric Morecambe

11 'My lawyers are
investigating'–
Rudolf Nureyev

12 'Don't call us, we'll
call You'–
Laurence Olivier

13 'Pure fantasy'–
King Kong,
Sunday Times

**A Message from
Ernie Wise:**
*'From the anlals of
literature we bring you
the cultural
foundations which
comprise the essence
of our civilization so
that your own mind
can flower like what
mine does with the
great thoughts of the
past present and
future'*

**A Message from
Eric Morecambe:**
'Buy them'

**A Message from
Antonia Fraser:**
*'Obviously no one
in their right mind…'*

Wise Book Club

4 'I did it differently'
Ezra Pound

5 'Horrifying'–
Eric Morecambe

How I made my 2nd pound
by Ernie Wise

Guide to Des O'Connor

9 'A fine work from a master of the English language'– Arthur Mullard

8 'Great'– Ernie Wise

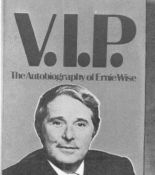
V.I.P.
The Autobiography of Ernie Wise

The Concise English Dictionarry
Words by Ernest Wise OBE

Absolutely FREE to each new member
The Wit and Wisdom of Eric and Ernie (26 volumes)

The Wit & Wisdom of Eric and Ernie Volume 1

My Hairy Friends by Eric Morecambe

Keep Fit with Eric

A Scrapbook of Cheque Stubs by Ernie Wise

and

THE COMPLETE DES O'CONNOR JOKE LEAFLET

14 'A simple tale of his legs; short and moving'– *Sunday Times*

15 'The lads nearly died of fright'–Don Revie

16 'An indispensable record of Ernie's chequered career'– Inland Revenue

Send No Money Now Just post this coupon tomorrow with your cheque for the price of **Just Twenty Books** And then select **ONE BOOK** per day which will arrive together with our representative to **Save you Posting** your money because he will take it from you. In this way you will build a **Magnificent Library** of **Thousands of Copies** of the same book.

I, being of sound credit, do hereby agree to all the terms and conditions of my membership as laid down in the other form drawn up by and exclusively seen by Eric and Ernie.
If not **COMPLETELY SATISFIED** I agree not to terminate my membership.

Name...

Address...

Annual Income ....

Instant Wisdom is yours.

Just present your WISECARD at any establishment and see them <u>grovel</u>.

some advantages of WISECARD:
- **Have people <u>queueing</u> for advice.**
- **Make Magnus Magnusson look <u>stupid</u>.**
- **Walk into <u>any</u> University.**
- **Know <u>everything</u> there is to know.**
- **Spend 5 minutes in Claridges.**

If you apply within 1 hour you will receive a free pair of "Clever" specs to start you off on your knowledge & Wisdom trip.

To receive a WISECARD you must answer the following questions correctly:

NAME _____

ADDRESS _____

Enough is not enough! You need MORE!

Eleven fabulous girls around the world have agreed to

Welcome this Card

If you are lucky enough to find one of these

Show her your Morecard. SHE WILL

Take you to her place to meet mother!

Teach you French cooking!!

Introduce you to her husband !!!

Take off Mike Yarwood !!!!

Do the dance of the seven dwarfs!

Just send £10 together with your

Own Girlfriend

to Eric Morecambe OBE and the Morecard will be yours.

Name..

Address..

Telephone number of your Own Girlfriend if between 18 & 25 ....

LESSON 1
Emerge dramatically from the Tunnel

TIPS from the TOP

Kevin Keegan learns from the Maestro

Above: Eric in grand manner. Mike Channon looks on enviously.
Right: All wrong. Never be less than sensational.

LESSON 2
Make the most of an Injury

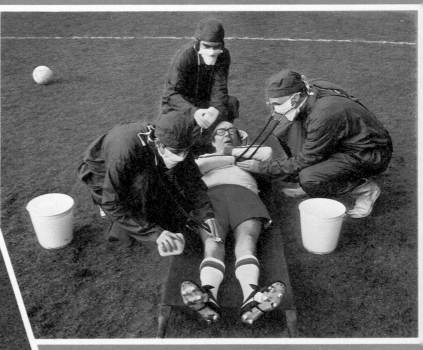

Left: Quite hopeless. Kevin wastes a golden opportunity.
Above: Eric in a life or death struggle.

LESSON 3 Whatever your feelings, don't show Dissent

Far Left: Graceful grovelling pleases the most hard-hearted ref.

Left: Kevin's little sign of displeasure will be noticed by the ref.

LESSON 4 Show affection to the Goalscorer

Below: A typical gesture lacking in imagination.
Right: 'My Hero.' Eric put warmth, feeling, romance into the celebration.

LESSON 5

Win a Psychological advantage at the Toss-up

The 'Tycoon Ploy.' Refuse to toss with notes of small denomination.

LESSON 6
Have your name taken with Good Grace

Below: When the ref asks your name, turning your back on him is impolite.
Far Left: Introduce yourself graciously and offer him your card.

LESSON 7
The Dummy

1 Eric, Wizard of Dribble
2 A quick shuffle of spectacles…
3 Kevin left helpless.

LESSON 8
Intimidate the Opposition

Right: Eric knows his worth.

Don't appear to be the Aggressor

Left: If you are compelled to exercise a little force…
Above: Make sure to blame your victim.

Taking the Penalty

Below: The goalkeeper is alert, poised…
Bottom: Kevin introduces a substitute. The goalkeeper remains alert, poised…

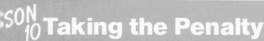

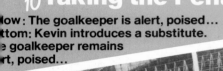

Be a Crowd-Pleaser

Above: Eric shows Kevin a song and dance tactic.

Ernie's Plan

THE atmosphere inside Number 11 was grim. A taut, nervous Chancellor paced up and down, because the floor sloped. The Governor of the Bank of England, summoned at short notice from a secret address unknown even to his wife, slept uneasily on the sofa. In the corner stood the tall, sinister figure of a bespectacled Arab, tossing fivers casually into the open fire.

There was a knock at the door and a pretty secretary ushered in an even prettier visitor.

'Mr Wise to see you sir,' said Miss Tress softly, and departed, pursued by the tall bespectacled Arab. Wordlessly the Chancellor motioned the newcomer to a chair, switched off *Kojak* and took an old exercise book marked *Budget, half way through* from a drawer marked *Keep off Wedgie*. He passed it to the small distinguished stranger who scanned it rapidly, expertly, pausing only to ask the meaning of 'insolvent'.

The Chancellor looked at him anxiously. 'What do you think of it so far?'

'Well Denis' (for it was he), said Ernie (for it was he), 'rubbish' (for it was).

The Chancellor burst into tears, grabbed a pre-packed suitcase labelled *Buenos Aires (please)* and made for the door.

'Not so fast young woman.' It was the voice of the tall bespectacled Arab who had returned unscripted and now stood arm in arm with the lovely Miss Tress blocking the exit. 'You forget that I, Sheik Yermoney, hold the keys and passports of the entire Cabinet, redeemable only on payment of the North Sea.'

'Moreover,' said Ernie, rising, though not very far, 'according to my rough calculations you owe the I.M.F. thirty billion pounds seven pee and Joe Coral six pounds fifty. My bill will be round in the morning with the heavies.'

The Chancellor collapsed like the pound. Then, he made a wild spring.

for Britain

'Don't go,' he cried, pinning Ernie to the floor. 'This is all your fault anyway.'

'All my fault Denis?' inquired Ernie, indignantly removing the pins and standing a little way up. 'Are you still beefing about my vast undisclosed and undeclared assets going on a numbered skiing holiday to Switzerland?'

'And look what it's done,' moaned the Chancellor. 'Everyone has left sterling, even the football team. Where's your love of old Albion? Have you no loyalty to Britain?'

'Nein.'

'No finer feelings?'

'I feel fine thanks.'

'No C.B.E.?'

There was a pause. Ernie, O.B.E., looked suddenly vulnerable; smaller; in fact almost invisible to the naked eye.

'You mean...?'

The Chancellor nodded.

'You won't go getting one for Eric?'

'You have my word as a friend of Harold Wilson'.

'Very well,' said Ernie, feeling with difficulty for his inside jacket pocket, for the movement was strange to him. 'How much do you want?'

'No little Ern,' whispered the Chancellor. 'It's not your money I want. It's your brain. Your rich, cash-intensive, liquid, surplus profitable brain. Tell me your secret,' he screamed suddenly, grasping Ernie by his shoulder pads and shaking him until the change rattled.

Ernie, visibly shaken, broke free and moved across the room to a grand piano where he composed himself.

'Alright Denis,' he said at length. 'I'll tell you.' He made a gesture. 'Since I was so low I have never in my life spent a penny.'

The Chancellor flushed. 'So,' he gasped. 'That's it. It's beautiful; classically, simply beautiful. We must do the same.'

'And quite by chance,' continued Ernie, 'I have brought with me a Master Plan.' So saying he produced from his trousers three new plays and a large piece of paper headed Master Plan.

He spread it on the floor. Then he scraped it off and the two men pored over it. The Governor of the Bank of England slept more soundly...

Ernie's Master

New Currency

A pleasure to have about the house; just as well because it can't be spent. Made entirely from soya beans, these luxurious notes and coins replace the boring old stuff. A national advertising campaign based on the slogan *You've never had it so what* will appear all over the place (which place to be decided). A new form of higher purchase will enable you to pay the highest prices without cluttering your home with what you've bought.

Fishing Limits

The 200-mile limit is to be rigorously enforced. British gunboats on wheels will patrol large areas of the Continent within these limits, and beyond if they get lost. By establishing a rightful claim to the banks of France, Switzerland and Germany, good fishing should be assured for years to come. Notes of small denomination will be thrown back until they get bigger. British housewives say they can get used to Swiss Francs and German Deutschmarks provided they taste like cod.

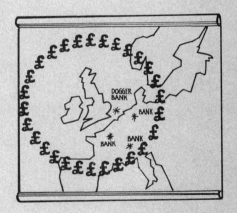

Sale of the Century

By answering a series of idiot questions you can buy a new antique for the price of an old one; a Life Assurance policy which expires when you do; and a selection of new releases from Pentonville. In addition you become eligible for Supplementary Benefits and get to grovel to Nicholas Parsons.

Sample Questions:

Easy for £1:   Would you like a cup of tea?
Is Bangkok a place or a nasty injury?
With one lump or two?

Medium for £3:   Name none of the Seven Wonders of the World.
Who wrote "Beethoven's Fifth"?
Who came fourth?

Impossible, for you! Who said, and in what 19th or 20th century novel, "Yes"?
Who except a lunatic would want a shot in the arm?
Why is free collective bargaini~ so expensive?

Plan

Premium Bonds

Ernie the versatile computer switches to a new programme. By selecting losers only, the government saves a fortune. At the same time everyone has the satisfaction of getting picked each week. The scheme is not only fun, novel and exciting; it is also compulsory.

The Golders Green Tax Haven

In a recent questionnaire thousands of very rich people, asked what they liked most, answered 'money'. This wonder-scheme will bring them here in droves, enabling us to milk the Sheiks and to have Johann Cruyff and Franz Beckenbauer as foreign reserves.

Concorde to South America

Who needs to get to South America in a hurry? Who can afford to fly Concorde Anyway? Answer – the same people!! If you are an International Criminal bored with passports, baggage checks and customs, this unique service could be your ticket to freedom.

FOR AS LITTLE AS £1,000,000 YOU TOO CAN ESCAPE JUSTICE

"TERRIFIC!" — MARTIN BORMANN

London's only Loo £100 a time

A mind-boggling device, making this a must for every tourist (average three times a day).

ARE

~~BORN~~

& RISE OF
AND WISE

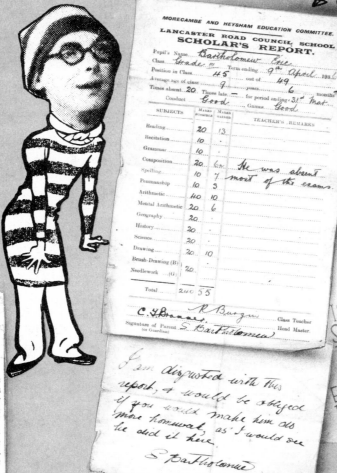

I am disgusted with this report, & would be obliged if you would make him do more homework, as I would see he did it here.

S. Bartholomew

"I'M NOT SUPPOSED TO BE ALL THERE!"
ERIC BARTHOLOMEW.
YOUTH TAKES A BOW. /1941.

Eric in caricature — aged 14

BOY WITH A FUTURE.

MAKES HIT IN SOLDIERS' SHOW.

Biggest hit in the variety interlude by soldiers at the Odeon cinema's sixth military night on Friday was made by a 13 years old Morecambe boy, Eric Bartholomew.

Odeon manager Mr. J. V. Sanders, in voicing thanks to the artistes, prophesied that the boy would go far in a stage career. By their applause, the audience showed they agreed.

In song, comedy and dance, Eric scored all along the line. There was not a trace of nervousness about him as he put over his numbers, which included the topical "Kiss Me Good-night, Sergeant Major."

TALENT-SPOTTING COMPETITION

Morecambe Boy First

A SHOW within a show was staged at the Arcadian Theatre on Saturday night when the final of the talent-spotting competition took place.

The standard of local talent was surprisingly high and the audience enjoyed it immensely. It was only after considerable difficulty that Peter Bernard, one of the artistes in the variety show, was able to select the three winners, who were chosen by the applause the audience gave them.

First prize was won by the Morecambe boy, Eric Bartholomew, whose singing of "I'm Not All There" really got the crowd. Pte Waters, who looked and sang like Bing Crosby, was a good second.

Stage appearance — aged 14

"M.M." DISCOVERY ON STAGE WITH HYLTON

INCLUDED in the Jack Hylton radio feature "Youth Takes a Bow" presented on Monday of last week at the Nottingham Empire, with Brian Michie as compere, was a 15 years-old Morecambe boy Eric Bartholomew.

Eric was one of the many "Melody Maker" readers who were recently auditioned at Hoylake, under Mr. Jack Fallen's auspices.

He competed on the Friday night, and entered the final on the Saturday, when he was chosen as one of the four to appear before Jack Hylton himself.

I happened to be present myself (writes Jerry Dawson) when Jack Hylton auditioned these four acts in Manchester, and at the time he was very impressed by Eric's versatility.

In dance, in song, or in burlesque this youngster had all the aplomb of a seasoned performer, and obviously with the necessary experience, here was a winner.

So once again, the "Melody Maker" helps to set on the road to fame a youngster of whom more should be heard as he matures. He is entirely self-taught and before entering for the "Youth Takes a Bow" competition, won innumerable local contests and has appeared on the stage at the Winter Gardens, Morecambe.

Eric Bartholomew is the name — watch out for it!

Heading the bill in "FRONT PAGE PERSONALITIES" is **FOGEL** in a brilliant mind reading act. While bubbling with fun right up to their fingertips are **the Pirates** "OH, YES THEY ARE." But **MORECAMBE and WISE** deserve HIGH PRAISE FOR AN ORIGINAL BRAND OF HUMOUR.

— Tony Hawes

YOUNGEST COMEDIAN

Morecambe Boy Broadcasts With Partner.

ERIC BARTHOLOMEW, 16 years old, only son of Mr. and Mrs. George Bartholomew, of 43, Christie Avenue, known professionally as Eric Morecambe, perhaps the youngest comedian on the stage, broadcast with his partner, Ernie Wise, aged 17, of Leeds, on Tuesday evening in the feature, "Youth Must Have Its Swing."

They were the youngest artistes in the programme. They told jokes in the American style. Ernie was supposed to do the "feeding" and Eric complained that he took the laughs!

Eric and Ernie on top of the situation, 1940

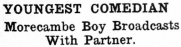

If you want to know about

Tegestology ASK Morecambe & Wise

They call themselves Tegestologists because they collect beer-mats. Tegestologists? That is their name for folk who collect them, and Morecambe and Wise are doing just that.

It is a very popular hobby with the two comics and takes them on many thirsty trails through pubs throughout the country. "Sometimes Eric likes green mats and other times he goes for red ones," said Ernie. "Personally, I think it is all a matter of taste!" Having added a new mat to their collection, they stow it away in their Tegestorium.

"'Teges' comes from the Latin for mat," says Wise learnedly. "I added the 'ology' bit," announces Morecambe, "because I like ologies—especially with pickled cabbage!"

The merry couple have come a long way in the entertainment world. Their clowning, both on the stage and before the television cameras, has made them one of the most popular double acts in the country. They get just as much fun as the audience out of their comic business. Once, for instance, Morecambe cut Wise's braces—whereupon Wise filled his partner's shoes with liquid glue. Both exploits had results which can better be imagined than related.

They agree on most things in life, including the cost

of the two suits a year which are ripped to shreds by Ernie. From time to time he gets so excited that he grasps his partner by the lapels and shoulders and pulls so hard that he invariably tears the seams. "We put the cost down to expenses," says the long-suffering Eric.

Like King Goon, Harry Secombe, Messrs. M. and W. worked as comics at the Windmill Theatre—only difference being that the two comics got the sack. They are not ashamed of the fact, though, for leaving this famous theatre was a lucky break for them. Soon afterwards they were booked at another well-known theatre and their salaries raised.

People often have difficulty in remembering who is who in the act. For the record. Eric is the owlish-looking character in glasses, Ernie, the one whom he exasperates. They have found show-business hard work, but they would not change their vocation for anything. Their recipe for success: "Rehearse, rehearse and keep original."

Eric is married to a former beauty queen. Ernie's wife is the former Doreen Blyth, of Peterborough. Ernie met Doreen, an ex-dancer, just after the war when they both toured the country in Sanger's Circus Variety Company. The two comics boast the same aim in life: "To own a bank—one each."

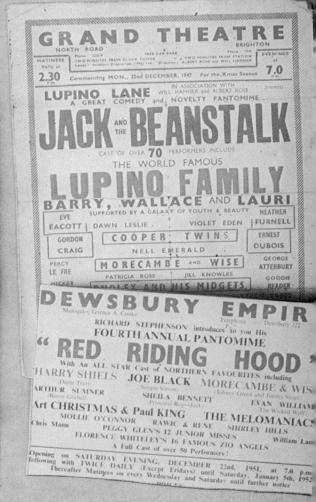

GRAND THEATRE NORTH ROAD BRIGHTON

MATINEES Daily at 2.30 — EVENINGS at 7.0

Commencing MON., 22nd DECEMBER, 1947 For the Xmas Season

IN ASSOCIATION WITH

LUPINO LANE A GREAT COMEDY and NOVELTY PANTOMIME

WILL HAMMER and ALBERT ROSE presents

JACK and the BEANSTALK

CAST OF OVER 70 PERFORMERS INCLUDE

THE WORLD FAMOUS

LUPINO FAMILY

BARRY, WALLACE and LAURI

SUPPORTED BY A GALAXY OF YOUTH & BEAUTY

EVE EACOTT	DAWN LESLIE	VIOLET EDEN	HEATHER FURNELL
GORDON CRAIG	COOPER TWINS		ERNEST DUBOIS
	NELL EMERALD		
PERCY LE FRE	MORECAMBE and WISE		GEORGE ATTERBURY
	PATRICIA ROSE	JILL KNOWLES	GOODIE READER
MICKEY	WORLEY AND HIS MIDGETS	

DEWSBURY EMPIRE

Manager—Terence A. Cooke — Telephone Dewsbury 322

RICHARD STEPHENSON introduces to you His

FOURTH ANNUAL PANTOMIME

"RED RIDING HOOD"

With An ALL STAR Cast of NORTHERN FAVOURITES including

HARRY SHIELS (Dame Trott) JOE BLACK (Simple Simon) MORECAMBE & WISE (Johnny Green and Jimmy Stout)

ARTHUR SUMNER (Baron Grabit) SHEILA BENNETT (Principal Boy—Jack) EVAN WILLIAMS (The Wicked Wolf)

Art CHRISTMAS & Paul KING MOLLIE O'CONNOR RAWIC & RENE SHIRLEY HILLS THE MELOMANIACS

Chris Mann PEGGY GLEN'S 12 JUNIOR MISSES William Lan

FLORENCE WHITELEY'S 16 FAMOUS ZIO ANGELS

A Full Cast of over 50 Performers!

Opening on SATURDAY EVENING, DECEMBER 22nd, 1951, at 7.0 p.m. following with TWICE-DAILY (Except Fridays) until Saturday, January 5th, 1952. Thereafter Matinees on every Wednesday and Saturday until further notice

Mrs Wise behind Mrs Morecambe overlooking a glassy-eyed Eric and friend

Eric and Ernie on the seafront at Blackpool.

"THE SHOW GOES ON"   SUNDAY 22nd MAY 1955

MORECAMBE & WISE

WISE: And now ladies and gentlemen it's my pleasure to
             introduce a young man who's name is rapidly becoming a
             household word. Too bad you can't say it in front of
             children. Eric Morecambe.

MORECAMBE: Thank you. Hey, I've only been in Manchester a few hours
             and I've met Milly Laura and Doris and Fido.

WISE: Wait a minute Fido sounds like a dog.

MORECAMBE: You think Fido is a dog. You should see Milly Laura and
             Doris.   Really I'm looking for a girl who does not
             drink, smoke, swear or go out with other men.

WISE: Why?

MORECAMBE: I don't know. Mind you I met a lovely girl here recently.

WISE: Did you really? How old was she?

MORECAMBE: I asked her that. I said "How old are you love?" she
             said "That's my business". Believe me I think she'd
             been in business a long time. I said "Watch out kid, I'm
             a go getter."

WISE: And what did she say?

MORECAMBE: She said "Go away, I'm looking for an already gotter"

WISE: Did you buy her a present?

MORECAMBE: I bought her a fur coat.

WISE: A fur coat?

MORECAMBE: Before I realized what had happened she snatched it
             from me hand, threw it in the wardrobe, locked it and
             said "Oh, you shouldn't have bothered." Then I bought
             her some roses for ten shillings a dozen. The florist
             said he raised them himself. I think he raised them
             from six shillings a dozen.

WISE: I think you should become a bachelor.

MORECAMBE: A bachelor?

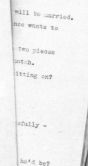

Cut here (let the poor man find out about the rest later)

Mona likes this bit - Lis

What the Artist missed

DROP THIS OR I'LL SUE! - DES!

I'll sell this bit to Old Spice –
v. Gogh

Drop the telly.
I hate
that show.
Cavalier

This will do!
WANT TO
PUTTA ME
OUTTA
BUSINESS?
Mario

Drop it Peter! Bad for the old image!

THE ERNIE WISE WALLET COLLECTION

1 The Ernest Wise Mark XX; believed currently in use by the inventor but seldom seen; no recorded sighting since 1949.

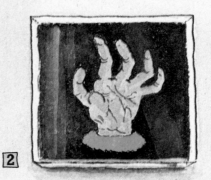

2 Hand of the thief who tried to extricate the Mark XX from its inventor.

3 The 'Friends of Harold Wilson' Wallet; bears the slogan 'Peer Inside'.

4 The world famous 'I've lost my Wallet Wallet'. Unseen in pubs everywhere, it responds to the phrase 'my round I believe'.

5 The miniature Kamikaze Wallet (made in Japan). Commits suicide when opened.

6 Henry VIII's famous 'Alimony' Wallet, loved by his surviving wives.

7 The famous Ernest Wise Mark II, winner of the Interpol award for total security. Contents unknown.

8 The Windmill Wallet, launched during the Second World War with the slogan "We Never Open." Contents unknown.

9 The World Wildlife Wallet, prized by naturalists as the habitat of the only surviving family of Short Fat Hairy Moths.

THE Morecambe & Wise Unit Trust

Bored Members
Eric Morecambe OBE
Ernie Wise OBE
John Stonehouse IOU
Ronald Biggs (Overseas)

The Team who Tipped
Vehicle and General ... Brentford Nylons ...
Scottish Daily News ... Slater Walker ...
IOS ... Rolls Razor ... Courtline ...
Simon Dee ...

Message from the co-chairmen:

Dear Shareholders,

In these troubled times we understand that some of you, and we emphasise only some (cousin Wilf has no complaints), have expressed anxiety about the performance of the Companies in which we, as experts, invest on your behalf.

First we would point out that we have never been slow to admit our mistakes. Only last year we issued a public apology for the over-enthusiasm of our forebears at the time of the South Sea Bubble in 1720. And we promised to re-pay every surviving investor the money he had lost; a pledge which, we are proud to report, was fulfilled immediately.

That venture was the first, but to critics we would emphasise by no means the least successful, of our enterprises. Our recent investment of a very great deal of your money in Southsea Oil was, to put it frankly, bluntly and openly, a minor geographical error. But we would remind you that a mere 180°flick of the compass would have sent us to where the oil actually was.

Now about Umbrellas (Sahara) Ltd. They folded. And so, through no fault of ours, did the Escort Agency and Punk Rock group formed by the monks of Buckfast Abbey. And we have very little to say about our involvement in the Patrick Moore School of Fashion and the David Coleman Course in a Wider Vocabulary.

It would be wrong to dwell only on our failures when there is much to say about our many triumphs. Other failures have been an expensive, but wholly patriotic attempt to colonize Russia, and the unfortunate collapse of State Secrets Ltd, which made the mistake of selling its product in department stores. Then there was The Channel Tunnel Ltd where, we have to say, we had no idea they meant to dig underneath BBC2.

All this should, we think, reassure you that we have your interests very much at heart. For ourselves we are taking a longish vacation on the Isle of Wight in a sheltered spot called Parkhurst. But keep buying.

Eric and Ernie

Eric & Ernie's daring pullout

Pin-up boys Eric and Ernie certainly show a leg in the morning, and lots of other things too! Lithe, lissom, with rippling muscles transplanted all over their amazing bodies, they love to swim, dance, ski, scuba dive and drink themselves under the table. They speak two languages (one each) and just adore travelling to far-away places which don't have extradition treaties. Life is good for these fun-loving guys who like nothing better than dressing up in their daring dark-grey suits and bowler hats. Leading members of the international propeller set they can often be glimpsed in exclusive haunts escorting fashionable models from Madame Tussauds. Winners of the Hercules Apollo beauty contest, a competition they organized themselves, they say their ambition is to settle down to a quiet family life and rule the world.

Lipsmackinthirstquenchinfingerlikinbodyglisninloinlurchintummytwistinnavelknottinfastlivinbonecrakinmuscleboundin

ERIC & ERNIE

MORECAMBE'S WAR DIARY

faced with such a horrendous future? I decide to change sides.

4 September 1939

British Army agree quickly. Special plane takes me to Germany. I crack a few jokes. Not a giggle.

*"Ver ist yor sense of humour?" I ask.
"A German joke ist no laughing matter," they reply.*

I am taken to see a small man who has a black moustache and a half-eaten carpet.

*"Haf you defected?" he asks.
I look at the cushion I am sitting on and say no.
He says, "No-von ist zo stupid as you, you must be a genius."*

I am made Head of German Intelligence.

31 December 1940

*Taken to see secret weapons, accompanied by dwarf policeman. Not much cop. I explain that I'm no good at keeping secrets but when he tells me what they do to blabbermouths I get suddenly rather good at it.
I am captured by a beautiful spy. I give her my name, rank and telephone number. She lets me go.*

21 June 1941

I am asked if I would like a ride in a U-boat. I refuse because they always sink. Meet Goering and Goebbels. They ask if we should open a second front. I say I'd rather open a second bottle. They say, "A second battle? Dat ist gut. Ve shall invade Russia tomorrow."

31 December 1942

My Russian campaign is going badly. I get all the blame. The Americans have joined in and we are definitely losing. I decide to change sides.

1 January 1943

The Germans seem pleased with my idea and a special plane takes me to England. I go to see Winston Churchill and introduce myself as Head of German Intelligence. I explain about my Russian campaign. He is very nice and gives me a two-foot cigar. He also offers me a place in his cabinet. Why does he want to shut me up in a chest of drawers? He tells me I have won the war and am the greatest Secret Agent in history. I say I must be since it was a secret to me. I become Head of British Intelligence.

1 June 1944

We meet to discuss D-Day. I explain I can't make it as I have some people coming to dinner. I am now Head of German and British Intelligence and I have become very important. They ask my advice about France. I tell them not to tell their wives. I learn a lot of details about the dangers of this particular trip and, as I am miffed about not being Head of American Intelligence, I suggest we send them over. I am made Head of American Intelligence, and I agree that the Americans (except me) and the British (except me) shall all go; and I agree to let them fight the Germans (except me).

8 May 1945

I have won and lost the war depending on how I look at it. Churchill very pleased and asks me to join his Party. I ask if it is evening dress or funny hats. I receive a letter from him telling me I am not Head of Intelligence anywhere anymore.

9 May 1945

I am now a civilian. What I need is a job in television. I am sure they will never beat Japan without me.

THE
WHITECHAPEL
MURDERS

A Tale of Sheerluck Holmes and Dr. Witsend

"beyond even his remarkable capacities"

I still recall in every vivid detail that chill, cheerless, foggy November night in the year of '82, or perhaps it was '92. My friend and companion Sheerluck Holmes was seated directly in front of the fire in such a way that I was entirely unaffected by its warmth. He was smoking his evil-smelling pipe and playing on his violin a tune of such difficulty that it was beyond even his remarkable capacities.

"something regal about her appearance"

Our attention was arrested by the arrival of a tall dark handsome cab, followed by footsteps along our stairs and the unmistakable sound of a loud insistent knocking at our door.

"Ah," said Holmes, his keen senses directed at once to this singular chain of events, "unless my senses deceive me we have a visitor who is, I deduce, a woman of quality who is not used to being kept waiting."

"Holmes," I gasped, for his almost telepathic powers never ceased to amaze me. "this is amazing."

"Perfectly simple," said he, above the din, "for the point at which the hammering is located indicates either a man of improbably small stature or, as I prefer to speculate, a woman. Again, only a lady of quality cries 'we command you to let us in' in a high-pitched voice. As for her impatience," he cried triumphantly, "she has even as I speak grown tired of waiting and has gone away."

"Wonderful," I exclaimed.

When she called again I let her in and we found ourselves confronted by an elderly lady with, I thought, something regal about her appearance. Without a word she handed me the Crown of England she was wearing on her head, and I, courteous as ever, relieved her of her purple cloak and purse. Holmes examined her with his magnifying glass.

"Pray tell us your business," he said, "for beyond the fact that you are called Victoria, you are a Queen by occupation and if I play my cards right I could get a knighthood out of this, I can deduce little from your somewhat disappointing appearance."

"We were wondering if," she paused, "you do not object to our use of the Royal We?"

"It's first on the left down the corridor," said Holmes.

"You are quite a card, Mr. Holmes," she replied with a royal flush. "We were wondering if you had heard of a series of dread crimes called the Whitechapel murders and the name of one they call," she paused again, "Jock the Ripper."

Holmes played a dramatic chord on his violin. Then he rose to his full height, as he always did when he stood up.

"So, little Queen, you've come to confess to these heinous deeds."

Our visitor roared with laughter. "We are not amused," she said. "The point is that our dear son Bertie, one day to reign as Edward VII and, by the Grace of God, to be the subject of a T.V. series, is suspected of the crimes. Our faithful gillie John Brown is behind these rumours, the silly gillie."

"Holmes examined her with his magnifying glass"

"Witsend," cried Holmes, "write the good lady a prescription to calm her nerves. Take it to the dispensing chemist, gracious madame, and you will find it indispensable."

"You are a loyal subject," said she, "unmask the true culprit and you will earn a sovereign's thanks."

"And perhaps," smiled Holmes, kissing the ring upon her fingers, "a sovereign's hand?"

"Nothing doing," said she, kicking him on the shins, "I'm off." I handed her her crown and cloak, retaining the purse as a small souvenir of this momentous encounter.

"At least I've got the ring," said Holmes, hopping about in some pain as she closed the door. "And now we also must be gone, for somewhere in London's East End lurks a desperate criminal waiting to be brought to justice." "Tell me, Witsend," he said, putting on his heavy overcoat, "what do you know of this case?"

"hopping about in some pain"

"Only that a terrible fiend has murdered countless harmless souls, that he operates on foggy nights and that he leaves the bodies of his victims foully mutilated."

"I rather think," said Holmes, taking off his heavy overcoat, "that we shall stay in tonight."

At that precise moment there was another knock on the door. My intrepid friend bade me open it and took up a position under the table.

I was startled to find an odd figure before me, clad in a tartan kilt, a butcher's apron and holding in his hand a street map of Whitechapel.

Holmes emerged from beneath the table.

"I rather think, Witsend, I shall now go out."

"Hoots ye won't," said the stranger. "I have come to warn ye, for your own good, not to meddle in the affairs of," he paused, "Jock the Ripper."

Holmes thought deeply for two seconds flat.

"There is much in what this gentleman says, Witsend. I perceive that the murderer, whoever he may be, will stop at nothing, not even me. Honesty compels me to admit that I am simply not expendable."

"Holmes emerged from beneath the table"

"Excellent reasoning," I cried, "but what should we deduce from the bloodstained knife of the very type used to perpetrate the Whitechapel Murders which our visitor holds in his hand?"

"I had not overlooked that," said Holmes, contemptuously retiring behind the curtain. "Nor have I failed to observe the singular stains upon his sporran. I have made some study of the curious marks which appear on sporrans in London and have written a small monograph on the 347 varieties I have isolated. These are unmistakeably from Whitechapel and I have no hesitation in pronouncing our intruder none other than Jock the Ripper."

"You clever fiend," gasped our visitor, bolting into the street. I made to follow him, but Holmes, wiser than I, restrained me with a rugby tackle.

"Make haste Witsend," he said, holding me securely, "or the villain will escape. We must act with all speed."

We acted *Hamlet* as quickly as we could and were halfway through *Othello* when Holmes suddenly slumped to the sofa, to which he was addicted, and closed his eyes as he always did following some giant drain upon his intellectual resources.

"The villain has eluded my clutches, Witsend, and his identity we may never learn. But of this I am certain: his new-found respect for my powers will ensure that never again will he resume his dreadful operations, and of this I will inform our gracious sovereign in the morning."

"But what's this?" I cried, picking up a silver locket dropped by our visitor in his haste. "It is inscribed *To John Brown from We!*"

"Witsend," said Holmes curling his lip disdainfully and putting it in his pocket, "such a commonplace name is clearly an assumed one, cleverly adopted to conceal the Ripper's true identity. Useless as a clue, of course, but I perceive it may fetch a few bob in the Portobello Road."

"Holmes, wiser than I, restrained me with a rugby tackle..."

Celebrity Squares

'We don't like people just because they're famous,' say Eric and Ernie, the People's Friends. 'They have to be rich as well.' This simple, homely philosophy has been their motto ever since, aged three, they caught a common cold. This so unnerved them that from then on they caught only the rarest and most exclusive viruses. Here are some of the illustrious characters who pop in and out of the Morecambe and Wise homestead to share a bag of crisps or a spin in the private sidecar.

Winning smiles for the Queen Mother.

A panic-stricken Napoleon with Vanessa Redgrave's Josephine.

With Richard Baker, the other newsreader.

Heart-throb Frank Finlay enchants Ernie.

Nina listens entranced as Eric sings

Ernie squares up to the formidable Oliver Reed.

A Statesman-like question from Lord George-Brown

Pete Murray asks a silly question

An encounter with Sean Connery, Mr Bond himself

With Andre Previn, alias Andre Preview

Opportunity knocks as Hughie Greene reads an Ern epic

A meeting of minds at the chimpanzees' tea party

THE VERY WONDERFUL JOKE PAGE

FAMOUS LAST WORDS

"Die my dear fellow?
That's the last thing I shall do."
Palmerston (we think)

"One of us will have to go."
Oscar Wilde (we think),
looking at repellent wallpaper

"This is no time to make new enemies."
Voltaire (we think),
asked by a priest if he rejected the Devil and all his Works.

"Aaaaaaaaaaaaaaaaaaah"
General Custer (we think)

"I am dying beyond my means."
Mark Twain (we think)

"I'm sure I can take it with me."
Ernie Wise (we know)

The Italian War Joke

It's about the new Italian tank. It's got four gears. Three in reverse and one forward in case the enemy attacks from the rear...

FAREWELL
TWO ARMS

THE WORST PUNS IN THE WORLD

'I'm just not very tall,'
said Ernie, shortly.

'Three new plays to write this morning,'
said Ernie, playfully.

'Ernie, I'm going to break you in two little pieces,'
wisecracked Eric.

'I hate fishing,'
he carped.

'I've lost that new job,'
he said, disappointed.

'Don't let that bull near me again,'
said the matador, cowed.

'Anything in the Honours List?'
asked George, peering hopefully.

'Then I grabbed my parachute and jumped,'
he explained.

The Hamlet Joke

Hamlet   *"Alas, poor Yorick, I knew him well."*

Horatio   *"He doesn't look a lot better now."*

THE GREATEST JOKE IN THE WORLD

There were two old men sat in deck chairs – One old man said, "It's nice out isn't it?– The other old man said, "Yes it is, I think I'll take mine out".

Join the dots

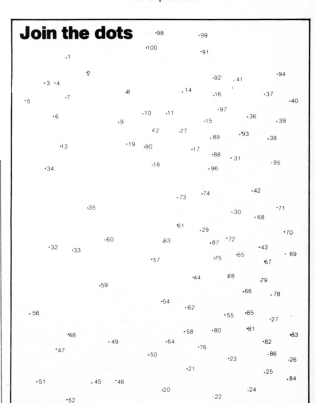

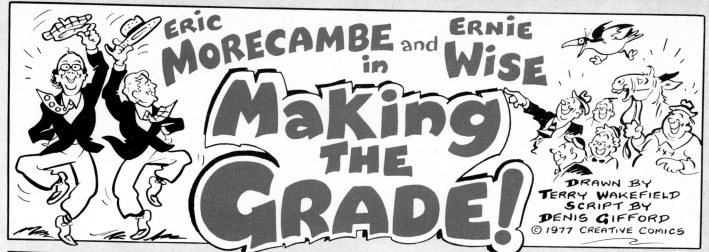

Eric and Ernie's CROSSWORD

ACROSS

1 If Lew invites you, you've made the . . . . . (5)
5 One of the famous short, fat hairy variety (3)
7 Oh Horror! For him you'll certainly have to pay (5)
8 Eric and Ernie's orders from the Palace (4)
9 An Ern play on the grand scale (4)
11 Like Ernie, a bit on the short side (6)
13 Oliver Twist's hungry request, or Eric without half his name (4)
14 Good-looking? Tall and dark anyway (8)
17 What actors do between engagements (and Eric's not averse to!) (4)
18 Eric's football team (5)
21 Could be tiny or big, but one of another pair of famous comedians (6)
23 Clever Billy to run a circus (5)
24 Those celebrated legs; short, . . . and hairy (3)
25 We thought she was just a newsreader till she discovered Morecambe and Wise (6)
26 Bring me . . . shine (3)

DOWN

2 What do you think of it so far? (7)
3 The singer Eric and Ernie most love to hate (3, 7)
4 All-knowing, just like Ernie (4)
6 The tall, good-looking one with the . . . . (7)
7 One like what Shakespeare and Ernie wrote (4)
10 Junctions – watched on television every night of the week (10)
12 Ray with the red breast (5)
15 Oscar Wilde recognized him as being important (6)
16 Famous actress who guest starred as Elizabeth I (6)
19 Sounds lordly but spells a great prize (6)
20 John, the singer pianist (5)
22 Can you see the join if Ernie wears one? (3)

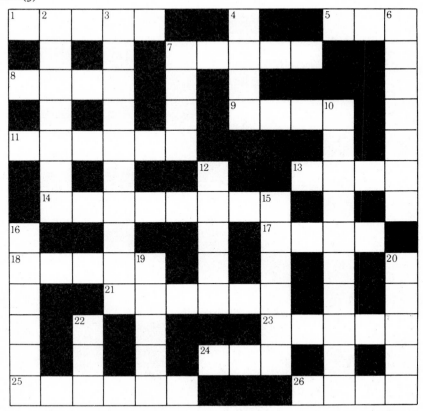

AND NOW

1. BRING ME SUNSHINE
   IN YOUR SMILE
   BRING ME LAUGHTER
   ALL THE WHILE

2. IN THIS WORLD
   WHERE WE LIVE
   THERE SHOULD BE
   MORE HAPPINESS

3. SO MUCH JOY
   YOU CAN GIVE
   TO EACH BRAND NEW
   BRIGHT TOMORROW

5

6

THE SONG

MAKE ME HAPPY
THROUGH THE YEARS
NEVER BRING ME
ANY TEARS

ET YOUR ARMS
BE AS WARM
AS THE SUN
FROM UP ABOVE

BRING ME FUN
BRING ME SUN
BRING ME
LOVE ♥

7

8

Eric Morecambe's SUN SIGNS

Aries

March 21–April 20

A bad year. Everyone you know is out to get you. Beware of strangers.

Cancer

June 22–July 23

You are ruled by Saturn, miserable planet which wi[ll] make rings around you. [A] good year for making a wi[ll]

Taurus

April 21–May 21

A fantastic time ahead, afoot, and in between for all tall handsome men in glasses called Eric Morecambe. Otherwise stay in bed, surrounded by next of kin.

Leo

July 24–August 23

Whatever you do, stay hi[d]den. I foresee only gloo[m] alarm and despondency f[or] you. During the year yo[u] will gradually disintegra[te] and probably drop dead.

Gemini

May 22–June 21

Stark-naked horror looms. Blue-eyed blondes over the age of consent are advised to contact tall dark Tauruses named Eric Morecambe. They won't be safe but at least they'll go down fighting.

Virgo

August 24–Septembe[r]

You are ruled (out) by Ju[piter] rising and Mars fa[lling] Look out for a bright [new] planet about to land or[top] of you.

for the Coming Year

Libra

September 24–October 23

I foresee a spot of bother with plague. You will be troubled by boils, locusts and earthquakes. Your only consolation is that next year will be worse.

Capricorn

December 22–January 20

A wealthy film producer will offer you stardom in a disaster movie. Unfortunately the disaster will happen before filming begins. It's safe to fly, but not by aeroplane.

Scorpio

October 24–November 22

They say there's always somebody worse off than you. Not true.

Aquarius

January 21–February 19

A bright start to the year. You will catch fire. Don't feel put out; you won't be.

Sagittarius

November 23–December 21

You have an inferiority complex, stemming from total inferiority. Avoid appearances on *Mastermind*. If on *Sale of the Century* you will remain unsold.

Pisces

February 20–March 20

A bad year for Pisces and Incomes. You will have no money problems, no clothes either. You will suffer from recurring bouts of foot and mouth disease, impeachment, and, like everybody else, Nicholas Parsons.

Eric and Ernie

on holiday

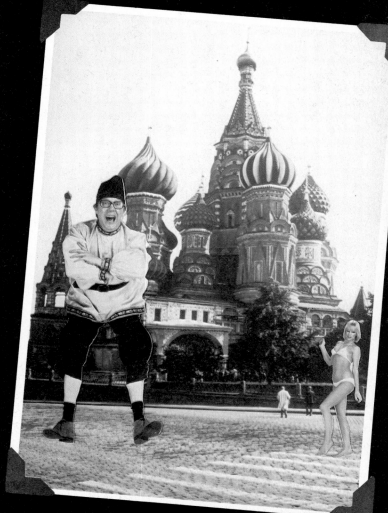

The TITLER

Jennifer at the London Season

The Season got off to a splendid start with a long-awaited wedding. Lots and lots of important guests turned up, including the bridegroom's irate wife and family. He was wearing a smart Moss Bros suit and seemed to be wearing rather badly.

Crufts was super! Doggy-people and people-doggies everywhere. Clement Freud, strengthened with extra thyamin, won first prize in the Parliamentary Whippet section. His owner, the unknown leader of the Liberal Party, earned a lucrative contract for feeding only on Wonderdog catfood for a year. 'Miaow', he barked a little later.

Perfect weather for Glyndbourne. How I loved the champagne on ice, the picnics on the lawns. I had a little of everybody's which added to the general fun, or at any rate mine. The evening was spoiled by some utterly horrid cabaret called, I think, Eel Traver-Tory, or some such person. Really! Next year I hope they let serious people get on with their own entertainment.

What fun at the Debs coming out! Lady Cynthia Havitt-Orf arrived with her debonair beau Claude St John de Vere Plantagenet Habsburg Bucket: Lady Gillian Tart-Crumpet was without her escort, fashionable man-about-town Ivor Profile who was somewhere out about town; in fact everybody who was anybody was there including Eddie Waring, who was up and under twenty times during the party.

The Queen was out in force to meet the English and West Indies teams at Lords. The sun shone brightly, obscured by heavy cloud and drizzle all day. Her Majesty asked Tony Grieg a technical question about his half-cock defensive prod and the ceremony was held up fully two seconds while he replied.

The Ascot Gold Cup was a glittering occasion. Lots and lots of important horses turned up. There was great excitement when the 100-1 outsider *Travel Dopefully* arrived in the Winners Enclosure because it came last.

The Garden Party at Buckingham Palace. How nice it was to be seen by so many notabilities. The Queen made lots of people feel at home by not asking them, so they stayed home.

Wimbledon was its usual self: strawberries, cream, and celebrities galore. There was tennis, too, and it was lovely to see all those athletic young men and women competing just for the sheer joy of the prize money.

The T.U.C. rally. Lots of pretty banners and simply *wonderful* placards. Also really *important* notabilities like Mr Hugh Scanlon (of the Shropshire Scanlons they tell me) and Mr Jones who apparently enjoys his social life so much he signed a contract for it with the Prime Minister, no less. How *nice* that there are still enough people with the leisure to put on parades like this instead of all being boring old working class.

Erica and Ernestine

Our wonder-girl reporter Angela managed to catch a glimpse of two ladies we don't often see up in Town. Erica and Ernestine are none other than twin sisters of the world-famous Eric and Ernie, respectively. "We don't often get out and about," they say, "because our brothers tell us we prefer a quiet life oop North in case we run into anyone they know in London." After meeting them Angela tells us she can see why.

How does it feel to be the sisters of the dynamic duo? "It feels lovely,"they say,"all over." Do they see much of their brothers? "Ooh yes, we never miss them when they're on the telly." Do the boys send letters? "Lots and lots. Every time somebody sends them a letter they don't want they send it straight on to us."

They left their 10 roomed flat in Burslem at 4·0am in the morning to catch the January Sales at Harrods, London's most famous Department Store. "We know it's only October but we like to be early," smiles Ernestine.

Erica, quietly spoken and tall, adores buying gifts for her twin brother and Harrods is the only place for her. "I've managed to buy his birthday present already," she says softly, "but I can't tell you what it is in case he reads this," (a sudden girlish laugh). I asked them how it felt to be the sisters of such an admired twosome. "Oooh, great," they whisper. "We had a loovly dinner ("lunch" to you) in the Harrods Caf ("coffee shop" to you). We ate ourselves silly," says Erica. "But it were worth it!" giggles Ernestine. "Back to the diet tomorrow!"

My Greatest Speech

Delivered to the Lord's Taverners by the new President (that's me) in the presence of the retiring President, Prince Charles (that's him): Deafening applause, in which I joined.

by Eric Morecambe

Your Royal Highness... Mr President, that's me, Mr Chairman... that's him... Fellow Taverners... and you people here...

As this is my first speech as your President... I might as well warn you now... if you don't laugh... it won't be my last...

May I, Sir, welcome you on behalf of the Taverners to this luncheon. May I also say how enjoyable the meal was... the menu was superb. As a matter of fact I'm thinking of taking it to Timothy Whites and having it made up. Good lunches like this are like jockeys legs... few and far between.

As I look along this table I see people... some of whom I've known for almost an hour and a half. And I say to myself 'Ernie'...oh yes even I get mixed up... I say to myself 'what a fortunate man you are... how lucky you are'. Then I say 'why?'... and then I say... 'I'll tell you why sunshine'... then I say, 'go on then', and I say to myself... 'you are a fortunate man... because you have no enemies... no enemies at all... you have a lot of friends who dislike you... but no enemies...'

Any President wants his term of office to be a successful one... and also having had his Royal Highness as our last President, and having, in show business parlance, to follow that... makes me feel a little nervous... the last time I was as nervous as this was when I was trapped in a lift with Larry Grayson.

Having had Prince Charles as a President was a wonderful thing for the Taverners... and I'm not just saying that because you're here Sir... I'm saying it because I'm a crawler.

We were going to have a surprise for you at this luncheon Sir. We were going to cancel the whole thing and not tell you.

Also we were going to have a six-foot cake wheeled into the middle of the room... and a naked girl was going to pop out. But when we took the cake out of the oven she didn't look too good... so we've scrubbed around that.

I would also like you all to know that as your President I will not be a yes man... when the Chairman says no I'll say no.

I asked the Chairman the other day... 'how many people work for the Taverners?'... and he said 'about half of them.'

Later in the year I shall be going over to the States to have a word with my opposite number, President Carter. We should get on well together as we have a lot in common. He grows nuts and I am...

Ernie is thrilled at me being President, because, as you all know, Ernie has a great infection for the Taverners. He was going to be with us... but unfortunately this morning he met with a slight accident. He was cleaning Lew Grade's car when his tongue ran dry. But Ern is a nice man. At the moment he is doing government work.. he goes out with sailors (no disrespect Sir). Ern was in the navy during the war... he has a great war record, it's George Formby's. *I'm leaning on a lamp* ...

Finally the war ended... Kaiser Bill was defeated so he came home. But back to realities.. so far as I'm concerned the idea of the Taverners is to make lots of money for our charities and at the same time to keep up the comradeship that exists in the Taverners. And to be able to make both money and friends through the game we all enjoy. Can't be bad...

I do realize that money is difficult to get at the moment... last year alone the cost of living shot up 30% a bottle. It shook Fred Rumsey... well, Fred likes a drink, and why not? He once held up a ship launching for three hours... wouldn't let go of the bottle. Anyway I digress...

I want my term of office to be as good, if not better than, any other President's... and with your help feel sure it will...

And now Sir; if I may ask you if you will accept from the Taverners a memento of your office and the time you have spent with us. This tankard, it's solid... solid what we don't know... but it has been inscribed with the Taverner's motto, Made in Hong Kong. It also has a list of girls' phone numbers from all over the world on the inside... the third one down's a knockout. If you ever ring that one and a man answers it'll be me.

On behalf of the Taverners may I be the first person this year to wish you a Merry Xmas and a Happy New Year.

Thank you Sir.

The Bank Robber
The famous Twopee

Madame Pompadour
The famous French cortisone

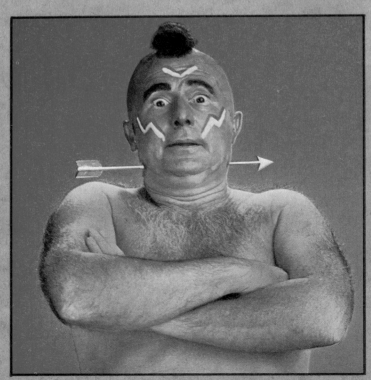

The Very last of the Mohicans
Me Red Indian Brave
Coward

The Pony Tail
I'm Ern—Ride Me

WIGS

The Patriot
Britannia rules OK!

The Des O'Connor Fright Wig
Here comes King Song

Kojak
'Completely undetectable'-Columbo

Superman
The natural look

GREETINGS FROM ERNIE

Ernie
~~The Lord Chamberlain~~ is

commanded by Her Majesty to invite

MRS WISE *and don't you forget*

to an Afternoon Party in the Garden of Buckingham Palace

on Thursday, the 13th July 1977, from 4 to 6 p.m.

Morning Dress or Uniform

Get Ill Soon

For YOU ...
and you alone

- [ ] Mrs Thatcher *
- [ ] Mary Whitehouse
- [ ] Fiona Richmond
- [ ] Basil Brush
- [ ] Danny la Rue
- [ ] Bionic Woman
- [ ] Angela Rippon
- [ ] Mrs Mao Tse-tung

Be my Valentine

* tick and pass on

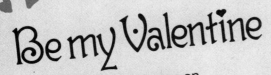

Merry Christmas from Ernie

(You owe me £20)

POST CARD

Thursday at the Bandstand.

De_ar all at number 22,¹⁰

We are having a ~~wonderful~~ *Wall Street* holiday here at ~~Clacton~~. The weather is sunny, *champagne* the sea warm and the food ~~quite~~ *very* passable. The other people in the guest house are ~~pleasant~~ *taller*, we've met a *fairly* nice couple from Luton. Just going for a walk on the prom so will close now. Regards to ~~Reg~~ *Marcia* and the kids.

Love ~~Babs~~
Ernie

TO: All at Number 10
(regards to next door)
London
W1

GREETINGS!

to my literary agent with 10% of my love

---

just
a little
reminder

24
SEPTEMBER

ERN'S BIRTHDAY

HAPPY

* Boxing Day!
  Christmas!
  Hallowe'en!
  Independence Day!
  Yom Kippur!
  Pancake Day!
  Orangeman's Day!
  Father's Day!
  Retirement!

from Ernie

* Delete where necessary

From Ernie with love xx

pst! Attach this card to your most expensive present

Ern's moving house

Ernie and Glenda

TOGETHER IN

Last Tango in Harpenden

'Love means never having to say I'm off'

1. Love's Tender Awakening

Ernie, the handsome wealthy aristocrat, finds true love.

2. Declaration

Glenda declares herself; she has always longed for a man she can look up to.

3. The Orgy

A supreme moment of unbridled passion.

4. Proposal

Glenda tells Ernie of her prospects and proposes marriage.

5. The Bedroom Scene

Ernie creates a fuss over the phrase 'for richer or poorer' but nonetheless the wedding takes place at a fashionable Cash Registry Office. Afterwards, a searing, passionate climax.

6. The Volunteer

War is declared.
Ernie implores Glenda not to go.

7. Confession

Glenda admits all. She has deceived Ernie, is
penniless and can offer him only love.

8. The Duel

Realizing they can live together no longer, Ernie
issues a challenge.

9. The Incurable Illness Scene

Missing with both shots, Ernie hits on a better
scheme.

10. Reconciliation

A postman's knock, a letter, and Glenda has
inherited her long lost uncle's fortune.
All is forgiven.

11. The Happy Ending Scene

They lived happily ever after.

CONTOUR

Holidays with a difference!

'7 Day Wonder' holiday-don't miss it!

No-<u>don't</u> miss this great offer of the Season! On the beautiful Costapakit. A holiday with a <u>difference</u>!

 Your Super Itinerary

AN ARTISTS IMPRESSION

- **Day 1.** Take off from a back garden in Harpenden in chartered 1918 Sopwith Camel. Arrive for Chip Butty Lunch (5 mins).
- **Day 2.** Start work at 6.0am after typical British Breakfast (chip butty). First foundation to be dug before lunch.
- **Day 3.** Lunch—10 mins. Digging all afternoon. Evening: sleeping bags made up in first trenches. The joy of sleeping in your <u>own</u> trench!
- **Day 4.** Breakfast (Typical British). More digging. Lunch. First Scaffolding erected before tea. Resting period of 10 mins.
- **Day 5.** FREE—at least for the first 2 hours. Afterwards more scaffolding and girders. Roof on and spend night 6 in the hotel <u>you</u> helped to build.
- **Day 6.** Souvenirs on sale on site.
  Breakfast on return flight to Harpenden (Chip Butty). Rest.
- **Day 7.** Rest—FREE OF CHARGE.

HOLIDAYMAKERS IMPRESSION OF THE ARTIST

*A subsidiary of M & W Holidays Ltd.

Acknowledgements

Thanks are due to the many people who have made this book possible: in particular to ourselves, Glenda Jackson, Kevin Keegan, the Arsenal Football Club, the Duke of York Theatre, and to everyone whose picture appears.

Art Director: John Rushton
Designed by John Rushton and Jacqueline Sinclair
Film Fun spreads by Denis Gifford
Illustrations by Jacqueline Sinclair, Rachel Beckingham, Helen Cowcher, Steve Kingston, Neil Collins, Chris Woolmer, Gordon Cramp, Angelo Cinque.
Photography by Philip van Deurs, Behram Kapadia, Graham Brown. Stylist: Jane Crow Make-up: Rhian Meakin
Studio and photographic work: Cara Chase, Jo Harris, Focus Photoset, Geoff Goode Photographics, Dupes Associates.

Glenda Jackson was photographed at The Duke of York Theatre. The set was for 'A Bedful of Foreigners', designed by Terry Parsons; Glenda Jackson's dress by Harvey Nichols.

Photographs in the book are reproduced by kind permission of the following: Associated Newspapers Group Ltd (68-9); BBC (48-9, 50-1); Camera Press (photograph by Patrick Lichfield) (endpaper); Douglas Dickens (63, bottom right); Robert Estall (62, bottom right); George Greenwood (centre spread); Keystone (64-5, 2nd row left, 3rd row left); Popperfoto (6, 64-5, 2nd row right); Rex Features (18, 64-5, top row left and centre, 3rd row centre and right); Ronald Sheridan (62 top left, 63 top left); Sport and General (64-5, 1st row right, 2nd row centre). Photographs of banks on pages 64-5 are by kind permission of the National Westminster, Midland and Lloyds Banks.

Printed in Great Britain by Redwood Burn Limited, Trowbridge & Esher
Illustration reproduction by Radstock Reproductions

GOOD NEWS	**BAD NEWS**
Cheer up Eric, the news is that everybody's wages are catching up.	Yes, to mine.
An English team has just regained the World Cup.	True. It was led by Ronnie Biggs.
Fifty thousand people stopped smoking last year.	They dropped dead.
Wonderful! Somebody has just won half a million pounds on the Grand National.	Terrific. I'm the bookmaker.
Here's one from the Middle Ages. It says people are living longer.	Right. The Spanish Inquisition just installed their new rack.
Passengers on a Jumbo Jet heard the pilot announce slight engine trouble. Not to worry, he said it would be OK if a few of the crew bailed out to lighten the load.	It was a recording.
Racquel Welch wants you to watch the late night film on television with her.	I've already seen it.
Alright, here's bad news then. The Chinese have landed on the moon.	Not so bad. All of them.